· NORTHWEST ·

KNOW-HOW

BEACHES

· NORTHWEST ·
KNOW-HOW

BEACHES

Rena Priest

Illustrations by **Jake Stoumbos**

SASQUATCH BOOKS
SEATTLE

Printed in China

SASQUATCH BOOKS with colophon is a registered trademark
of Penguin Random House LLC

26 25 24 23 22   9 8 7 6 5 4 3 2 1

Text: Rena Priest
Illustrations: Jake Stoumbos
Editor: Jen Worick
Production editor: Bridget Sweet
Designer: Tony Ong

Library of Congress Cataloging-in-Publication Data
Names: Priest, Rena, author. | Stoumbos, Jake, illustrator.
Title: Northwest know-how : beaches / [text by] Rena Priest ;
   [illustrations by Jake Stoumbos].
Other titles: Northwest knowhow, beaches
Description: Seattle : Sasquatch Books, [2022] | Series: Northwest know-how
Identifiers: LCCN 2021024207 | ISBN 9781632174086 (Hardcover)
Subjects: LCSH: Beaches–Northwest, Pacific.
Classification: LCC GB459.4 .P75 2022 | DDC 917.904–dc23
LC record available at https://lccn.loc.gov/2021024207

ISBN: 978-1-63217-408-6

Sasquatch Books
1904 Third Avenue, Suite 710
Seattle, WA 98101

SasquatchBooks.com

FSC
www.fsc.org

MIX
Paper from
responsible sources
FSC® C169962

For Spark

CONTENTS

xi   *Introduction*

Semiahmoo

2   Semiahmoo Spit

The San Juans

9   Eagle Cove Beach
10   Fourth of July Beach
13   English Camp
14   Lime Kiln Lighthouse
19   Crescent Beach Preserve
20   Doe Bay

Whidbey Island

24   Deception Pass State Park

29   Coupeville

30   Ebey's Landing

Camano Island

36   Cama Beach

The Olympic Peninsula

40   Dungeness Spit

43   Glass Beach

46   Fay Bainbridge Park

Seattle Beaches

50   Richmond Beach

53   Carkeek Park

56   Golden Gardens Park

59   Myrtle Edwards Park

60   Alki Beach

The Washington Coast

64   Rialto Beach

67   Ruby Beach

70   Kalaloch Beaches

73   Copalis Beach

74   Long Beach

The Oregon Coast

80   Wreck of the *Peter Iredale*

85   Seaside Beach

86   Cannon Beach

91   Manzanita

94   Depoe Bay

97   Cobble Beach

98   Agate Beach

103   Hobbit Beach

104   Heceta Head Lighthouse

109   Sunset Bay State Park

111   *Safety and Guidelines*

116   *Activities by Area*

119   *Resources*

121   *Acknowledgments*

122   *Index*

PLUS . . .

4   The Story of Raven and Salmon Woman

16   Silence from the Deep

26   The Maiden of Deception Pass

32   Songs on the Salmon Scale

44   Beach Glassing

54   Flotsam and Jetsam

68   Beach Party

76   The Changer and the Gossips

82   Shipwrecks

88   Dramatic Geology of the Oregon Coast

92   Beach Glass

100   Beach Fire

106   Lighthouse Lodging

INTRODUCTION

Many of my earliest and best memories take place on
beaches. Every year from Mother's Day to Labor Day,
tribes of the Pacific Northwest gather on beaches to
watch or participate in intertribal canoe races. Paddlers
begin training in early spring, and as a child, I often
accompanied my mother during canoe practice.

Sometimes I got to ride along. As we sped across the
waves, I would dip my hand over the side and watch as
the water leapt up around my fingers, then swirled away
behind us. The downside to riding in the canoe was that
I had to be very still so that we didn't tip. This is a big ask
for a small child, so I usually opted to sit on the beach and
watch the paddlers grow small as they went away, then
grow large again as they returned.

During all that time onshore, I discovered an endless
number of things to do on a beach. You could tip over
rocks and watch the tiny crabs scuttle away down into
the darkness. You could skip stones and look for agates,
or beach glass, or eagle feathers. If there were other children, you could build driftwood forts.

Eventually, we moved from the western shore to the
eastern shore of our reservation. There was a new beach
with new diversions. For starters, the tide went way,

waaaaay out—so far out that it seemed you could walk across the bay to get to town on the other side. I once walked with my brother and sister and a bunch of cousins to catch up with the water's edge. It must have taken us hours. We had to race the tide back in. It was a thrill and a terror to have salt water pooling at our heels, though I think we were more likely to be carried off by an eagle than to be sucked out into the bay.

All summer long we spent entire days playing on the beach. We would pack a cooler full of snacks and head for the water. We would build a fire and roast marshmallows and hot dogs. Sometimes during a minus tide, the adults would join us and have a volleyball game out on the tide flats. If we were lucky, the high tide would spit out a giant log into the bay. We would try to clamber on top of it and ride it, pretending it was a whale, a surfboard, or the *Titanic*.

Though I don't spend as much time at the beach as I did when I was a child, I still make regular visits to beaches near my current home and short day trips to beaches around the Pacific Northwest. The happiness and peace of these places is a treasure. Rain or shine, the shoreline is a place of magic and majesty. I invite you to visit one or many of the beautiful public beaches in this book and soak up some of that happiness that dances across the waves.

Land Acknowledgment

Since time immemorial tribes have thrived along the shores of the Salish Sea. We have celebrated rich cultural traditions and customs. We have enjoyed a vibrant and sustainable trade economy. Our beaches have long been places of reciprocity, where gifts are exchanged between the creatures and the people of the sea. The glittering waterways have provided us with life-giving sustenance, acted as our highways so that we might connect, and filled our spirits with awe so that we might always hold the beauty of our homelands in the highest reverence.

Many of the beaches in this book offer interpretive exhibits along trails and at viewpoints. Some outline the history of European settlement, while others give details on how to interact with the area's biological diversity. As you enjoy your time in these beautiful places, please also acknowledge that for thousands of years these sites have also been special, and even sacred, to tribes.

I invite you to feel profound gratitude for the land and water—to experience these places with the same love and reverence felt for them by their original inhabitants. I invite you to let your feeling for these places shape you. I invite you to carry love for this beautiful Earth into all the spaces you inhabit and to interact with them accordingly.

Customs and Traditions

When a visiting tribe arrived on their neighbor's shores, a delegation was sent to greet them. Visitors would request permission to come ashore, and the leader of the greeting party would invite them to rest and take nourishment with respect for the customs of the land. This protocol is still practiced during the annual intertribal canoe journey, which occurs every summer, drawing participants from tribes throughout Washington and British Columbia. Canoe landings are open to the public, and everyone is invited.

In addition to the time-honored traditions celebrated by tribes, new traditions are also observed. Beaches serve as venues for live music, kite festivals, sandcastle-building contests, clambakes, company picnics, weddings, polar bear plunges, and all sorts of other delightful occasions. Many of the beaches described in this book feature facilities that support an array of events. A handy index at the back of the book groups beaches by their features and activities.

How the Book Works

In the following pages you'll get a snapshot of the best beaches in Oregon and Washington. Beaches are grouped by region and run from north to south (except on the Olympic Peninsula). Each regional section includes an introduction that briefly describes history, points of interest, and common traits connecting a region's beaches. Individual beach descriptions highlight "know-how," so you can feel like a savvy local.

While this is not an exhaustive guide, you'll find helpful information such as laws and safety guidelines, as well as some fascinating history, fun facts, poems, and legends. Ever wonder about the best places to launch a kayak, harvest clams, or gather beach glass? This book has recommendations for all that and more. Read on, and I'll even tell you where to hear the orcas sing.

Semiahmoo Spit

Semiahmoo

~

SEMIAHMOO

2   Semiahmoo Spit

Semiahmoo Park is a biologically rich site located in the northwest corner of Washington State. From Semiahmoo Spit's outer shore, you can see the high-rises of the Canadian city of White Rock. At the northern tip you can see the Peace Arch, glowing white and marking the international boundary between the United States and Canada.

Semiahmoo Spit

The slender arm of Semiahmoo Spit runs along the western edge of Drayton Harbor, forming part of what is referred to as the Northwest Necklace. All along the shores of Drayton Harbor, you will find enjoyable ways to spend your visit—a resort and spa, a golf course, a harbor, a museum, and of course, a beautiful beach.

The beach hosts thousands of migrating birds every year, and the tidelands are home to an array of species. The waters are calm and clear, and the beach is a delightful place to walk. The trees are dotted with bald eagles.

The main buildings here are vestiges of the days when the Alaska Packers Association operated one of the world's largest fish canneries. Prior to that era, Straits Salish tribes occupied this area for hundreds of generations, enjoying the beautiful surroundings and access to abundant food sources.

KNOW-HOW: Interpretive exhibits are on display throughout the park. One such presentation includes a totem pole carved by renowned Lummi carver Morrie Alexander. It tells the story of Salmon Woman and Raven.

The Story of Raven and Salmon Woman

So very long ago, when Raven was out on the water, a thick fog came up around him. No matter which direction he went, the fog was like a wall. Just when he'd given himself up for lost, a beautiful woman appeared beside him. She took the spruce root hat from his head, and before he could protest, she held it out and the fog disappeared into it. Grateful, Raven asked her to marry him. She agreed and went to shore with him.

One day the woman asked Raven to go to the beach and fill his hat with water. When he returned, a shining fish was swimming inside. The woman then instructed Raven to build a smokehouse. "Wait four days," she said, "then go back to the water." On the fourth day, he found the waters teeming with fish. "These are called Salmon," said the woman. "They will provide you nourishment and health." Raven thanked her and called her Salmon Woman.

In the seasons that followed, Raven devised all kinds of ways to catch and prepare the fish. Soon he began to use the salmon to grow wealth. Instead of enjoying them for nourishment and health, he caught them to sell. As he grew more prosperous, he paid less attention to Salmon Woman, forgetting that it was she who'd brought him this gift that had made him so rich.

One day she'd had enough. She decided to leave and set off down the beach. When Raven called out to her, she turned to face him, and before his eyes she became a wisp of fog that drifted out over the water. Raven heard a sound like a rushing creek coming from the smokehouse. When he turned, he saw the salmon had come back to life.

In an instant the fish rushed past him, splashed into the water, and swam away—leaving Raven as poor as he'd been before Salmon Woman brought him such good fortune. But salmon had been created for this world, and so they return each year to provide nourishment, but not riches. Raven will tell you that if things are not kept in balance—if salmon are used for money not health—they may disappear forever.

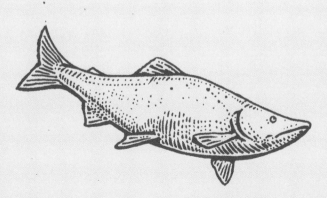

THE SAN JUANS

9   Eagle Cove Beach

10   Fourth of July Beach

13   English Camp

14   Lime Kiln Lighthouse

19   Crescent Beach Preserve

20   Doe Bay

This secluded archipelago has a wealth of serene beaches to explore. Sheltered by Vancouver Island, the waters here are often calm and perfect for swimming or paddling. Because it takes some effort to reach the islands, you'll find that beaches here are less crowded than mainland beaches and more pristine.

The two islands with the most amenities for visitors are San Juan Island and Orcas Island. It's hard to imagine that there could be much diversity between the six beaches outlined in the following pages, but you'll find that each beach offers a distinctly unique experience. From May to September the ferries tend to fill up fast. Reserve early to avoid disappointment.

Eagle Cove Beach

The light here at midday is stunning, and it feels as though the sun is shining just for you—and maybe it is. It's possible on any given day to have the place entirely to yourself. If it's warm out, you'll find it impossible not to swim. The beach is sandy at the base, with small rocks and driftwood at the high tide line. After your swim, you can choose a piece of driftwood to perch upon and listen to the delightful alto whoosh of waves, rhythmic and varied like they're playing you a song. This is the perfect place to spend a lazy afternoon.

KNOW-HOW: A small parking lot provides access to the trailhead for a short five-minute walk downhill. Your reward will be this treasure of a beach, running along a small cove and nestled at the base of a cliff. If you listen carefully, you could well hear eagle chirps.

Fourth of July Beach

Fourth of July Beach runs along the northern edge of American Camp and offers a beautiful view of the Salish Sea. The seas here are usually amiable and calm. On a windless day the water shines like glass, and a rare stillness engulfs this quiet place, making it an optimal location to enjoy meditative bliss or a nice swim in the crystal-clear salt water.

The beach is composed of small rocks, gravel, and driftwood. West of the trail from the parking lot, you'll notice large rock formations resting along the beach. These offer a nice place to hunker down for a picnic while taking in the sights and sounds.

KNOW-HOW: In the foliage that runs along the beach, you may see fox trails or even foxes. These adorable animals are habituated to people, so they may seem very approachable—but give them their space. They're also one of the many reasons that it's vital to carry anything out that you may have brought along for a picnic.

English Camp

This historical park is best enjoyed by hiking the extensive trail system and reading the many interpretive exhibits outlining the history of English Camp. Between 1860 and 1872 this area served as a British military base. Vestiges of this brief era are still evident in the buildings and the classic English garden at the water's edge.

Before British occupation, this area was a Lhaq'temish (Lummi) village. As you read about the English soldiers who stopped here for a moment in history, please also keep in mind the Indigenous peoples who made their lives along these shores for hundreds of generations.

KNOW-HOW: Due to vulnerable coastal habitat, beach access is limited throughout most of the park, but if you follow the path north along the water to Bell Point Trail, you'll eventually come to a picnic table, which marks a short path to a narrow stretch of beach at the northern edge of Garrison Bay.

Lime Kiln Lighthouse

The waters surrounding the Lime Kiln Lighthouse are a favorite of the much-beloved southern resident killer whales. So much so that the Whale Museum has installed underwater microphones near the lighthouse so that visitors might be able to hear the underwater sound of pod songs and the sonic clicks orcas use to hunt and echolocate. The Whale Museum has operated a research station from the lighthouse since 1983.

KNOW-HOW: When you visit be sure to stop by the lighthouse and read the Whale Museum's nearby display with information on the marine life in the waters below. If you push the silver button, you can listen to what it sounds like beneath the waves. Because of the abundant marine life in these waters, this is also an excellent place for divers and snorkelers.

Silence from the Deep

How do we mistake desolation for peace?
When orcas no longer sing will we grieve?
Waves say "hush" along the beach.
Under the waves, there is no reprieve.

When orcas no longer sing will we grieve?
Each generation dwindles in number.
Under the waves, there is no reprieve
from human noise, pollution, hunger.

Each generation dwindles in number.
The world is a mirror of our hearts. Look away
from human noise, pollution, hunger.
Everything is endangered or going extinct.

The world is a mirror of our hearts. Look away
so as not to see how under the waves
everything is endangered or going extinct.
When orcas no longer sing, will we see?

Will we see how under the waves,
the waves that say "hush" along the beach—
when orcas no longer sing, will we see
how we mistook desolation for peace?

Crescent Beach Preserve

This protected site is a nature lover's delight. The shore-line is only one small feature of the rich surroundings that comprise a recognized nature preserve. In addition to the beach, the preserve contains a large bulrush marsh and an impressive stand of quaking aspens.

Together, the intertidal zone, freshwater wetlands, and upland forest provide habitat for shellfish, birds, frogs, salamanders, river otters, and a plethora of other wildlife. The beach above the oyster beds is open to the public during the daytime, and if you decide you'd like to get out onto the waves, kayaks are available for rent just a stone's throw away.

KNOW-HOW: There is no camping, and the paths through the preserve are for pedestrian access. Pets must be leashed to protect habitat and wildlife.

Doe Bay

The gorgeous beach is excellent for swimming and also acts as one of the only publicly accessible beaches on the east side where you can launch a kayak or portable boat. Guided kayak expeditions are available twice daily and can be booked through the Doe Bay Resort.

Foodies, take note: The Doe Bay Café is a culinary treasure featuring flavorful local seed-to-table cuisine. Enjoy a spectacular meal with a stunning view and follow it up with a barefoot stroll along the water. The sand here is nice underfoot, and the shallow water is perfect for wading. The bay is shaded by Douglas fir and madrone trees, which add to the restorative vibe.

KNOW-HOW: There are drive-in campsites which include showers, a kitchen, and a hot tub. For those wanting a more remote camping experience, walk-in sites with breathtaking views are set a world away despite being a short walk from a parking area. For glampers, there are yurts and domes. All sites can be reserved through the Doe Bay Resort website. Fires are not allowed at campsites or on the beach, but the resort provides details on areas where a fire may be enjoyed. Live music is a notable feature of the summer here, so take that into account when planning your visit.

WHIDBEY ISLAND

24   Deception Pass   30   Ebey's Landing
State Park

29   Coupeville

Whidbey Island is the largest island in Washington State. With so much shoreline surrounding it, the island boasts some of Washington's most spectacular beaches. You can reach Whidbey by ferry, but one of the best ways to visit is by taking Washington State Route 20 across the bridge over Deception Pass. This grand gateway to Whidbey is one of the most scenic places on Earth.

The beaches highlighted in the following pages are on the northern half of the island. If you love what you see, be sure to continue south to visit Double Bluff County Park, the Deer Lagoon bird sanctuary, and the Langley Whale Center.

Deception Pass State Park

This is the most visited state park in Washington, and for a good reason. Here, beach lovers will be awestruck by the dramatic beauty that abounds along the park's 77,000 feet of saltwater shoreline. At the eastern tip of Pass Island, you can watch the tide rush by at 8 knots (9.2 mph), creating ornate whirlpools and roiling eddies.

Cornet Bay offers a boat launch, and kayak rentals and tours can be booked in Bowman Bay. Rosario Beach features tide pools and picnic areas, while long, leisurely strolls and breathtaking sunsets are highlights best enjoyed at North Beach and West Beach. The park also provides access to three separate campgrounds with more than two hundred campsites and 38 miles of hiking trails.

You can follow the Goose Rock Summit Trail to access Whidbey Island's highest point, with stunning views in all directions, or hike Hoypus Point to pass through old-growth trees. Hoypus Point Natural Forest Area trails allow bikes and horses as well as pedestrians.

KNOW-HOW: Be prepared to brave the crowds during peak season. Parking requires a Discover Pass and is not always guaranteed. Arrive with a "go with the flow" mentality, and you're sure to be delighted with where your explorations lead.

The Maiden of Deception Pass

A totem pole at Rosario Beach looks out over the water, inviting visitors to learn the story of the Maiden of Deception Pass. A beautiful maiden named Ko-kwal-alwoot was out gathering shellfish with the other girls of her village. She reached into the water to pick up an oyster, and she felt someone take hold of her hand.

She looked into the water and saw the face of a handsome young man. It was one of the people who live under the waves. He said to her, "Don't be afraid. I just want to look at your beautiful face." He let go of her hand and later came ashore to ask the maiden to be his bride and live with him in the sea. The girl loved her people and didn't want to leave, so she said no.

The young man and the people from under the sea were offended. They no longer shared their gifts of clams, oysters, and fish. The land people began to go hungry, and because she loved her people so, the maiden agreed to the union on the condition that she could return home to the land for visits.

The maiden found she was happy in her life under the sea, and it became increasingly difficult for her to be on the land. Her people said, "We truly love you, but we understand that the sea is your home now. We see it's hard for you to be away. You don't have to come back."

But she is always there, watching over her people. Her hair is the kelp that sways in the tide.

Through the maiden, the covenant of reciprocity between the people of the land and the people of the sea has been upheld. Today, the gifts of the sea are disappearing again. This means that we must honor our connection with the people under the sea and take care of these waterways to ensure their health and well-being.

Coupeville

From the historic wharf of this picture-perfect town, you can see the floats where Penn Cove mussels are grown for restaurants throughout the region. You can access a small public beach via stairs conveniently nestled beside a bakery on the main street overlooking the cove. Stop in for a cardamom roll, marmalade pinwheel, or some other tasty treat to enjoy as you stroll along the water's edge.

KNOW-HOW: In May of each year the Penn Cove Water Festival features tribal canoe races, music, dance performances, vendors, and delicious food.

Ebey's Landing

This long stretch of rocky beach sits at the bottom of a cliff overlooking Admiralty Inlet. There is a meditative stillness about this beach. It's a great place to relax and clear your mind. It's also a favorite among fishers. If salmon are running, you'll likely see anglers trying to catch a fresh fish for dinner. If you're looking for more than a low-key day at the beach, you can work in a bit of cardio with a hike up the gently sloping path that climbs the cliffside. At the top, rest on a bench and enjoy the sunset or take in the sweeping views of the Salish Sea.

KNOW-HOW: Along your walk you will encounter historical farms and houses built by European settlers. The lighthouse at Fort Casey is situated just a few miles south of Ebey's Landing. These historical landmarks offer an excellent opportunity to learn about local history. Before settler-occupation, this area was the site of a Skagit village. Archaeologists have unearthed artifacts on Ebey's Prairie dating back ten thousand years.

Songs on the Salmon Scale

A salmon is a song sung in rounds,
a series of concentric circles
like a raindrop in the sea,
rippling out and returning.

A series of concentric circles,
a chorus and a verse
rippling out and returning
in a shining body of treasure.

A chorus and a verse,
a hero, home from adventure
in a shining body of treasure
bearing gifts from the deep,

a hero home from adventure
like a raindrop on the sea
bearing gifts from the deep,
a salmon is a song sung in rounds.

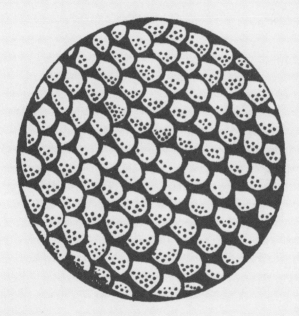

CAMANO ISLAND

36   Cama Beach

Camano Island is just a hop, skip, and jump from Interstate 5, but it's just far enough away from everything else to preserve the integrity of its environmental splendor. Though just a short drive from Seattle, the island feels off the beaten path. A bridge connects the island to the mainland, providing easy access to beaches and trails. This island is an outdoor enthusiast's delight.

Cama Beach

"Everybody needs beauty as well as bread, places to play in and pray in, where nature may heal and cheer and give strength to body and soul alike." This quote by naturalist John Muir appears at the top of an interpretive exhibit overlooking the beach. It's the perfect summary of why you'd want to visit this beautiful place and why local tribes used the beach as a village site for thousands of years. The Tulalip tribe still actively lived here at the time of the first European arrivals.

You can see why it is beloved by the region's original inhabitants. In addition to being scenic, this was a good place to live due to the abundance of fish, shellfish, and berries. In the 1800s the site served as a logging camp. Then in the 1930s, it became a resort. Remnants of that era are still evident by the camping cabins that line the shoreline.

KNOW-HOW: This park is also home to the Center for Wooden Boats, a museum, and a café. Cabins are available for rent, but book well in advance, as it can be hard to secure a reservation. A Discover Pass is required to park, but there are fifteen-minute parking areas if you only plan to make a short visit.

THE OLYMPIC PENINSULA

40   Dungeness Spit   46   Fay Bainbridge Park

43   Glass Beach

With the majestic Olympic Mountains as their backdrop and limited access, these beaches provide a feeling of being a world away from everyday life. To reach Dungeness Spit and Glass Beach, you can take the ferry from Coupeville across Admiralty Inlet, or you can take the ferry to Bainbridge Island out of downtown Seattle and drive north to Fay Bainbridge Park. It's truly remarkable how a journey across the water can provide an instant sense of stepping away from it all. If you plan to take the Coupeville ferry, reserve your spot in advance.

Dungeness Spit

Jutting 5.5 miles into the Strait of Juan de Fuca, Dungeness Spit is the longest natural sand spit in the United States. Sediment eroded from nearby cliffs gathers at the end of the spit, causing it to extend its reach by 13–15 feet per year.

The New Dungeness Lighthouse has steered boats clear of the sandy point since 1857. In more recent times, the beacon has become an attraction for beach hikers. If you plan to make the 11–mile round-trip journey, check the tides before you go and give yourself plenty of time to enjoy the walk.

Dungeness Spit is also a wildlife refuge, providing vital habitat to more than 250 species. With so much biodiversity, the site is a bird-watcher's paradise and a nature photographer's delight.

KNOW-HOW: If you plan on traversing the length of the spit, be sure to wear comfortable shoes and bring a water bottle and snacks that you can pack out. There are restrooms and a picnic table at the lighthouse but otherwise no facilities, so hit the restrooms in the trailhead parking lot before you step out onto the spit.

Glass Beach

There is a type of beachcomber whose heart sings at the sight of a bright pebble of glass worn smooth by time and tides. If you are such a type, Glass Beach will be at the top of your list of beaches to comb. It's a bit of a hike to reach the best specimens, but the consensus is that it's well worth it.

Seasoned beachcombers advise that when smaller nuggets appear sporadically along the shoreline, you should charge onward until you reach McCurdy Point, the beach glass jackpot. Even if you're not a beachcomber in search of glass treasures, this place is so novel and the walk so lovely that it's worth the trip.

KNOW-HOW: Mind the tides! You should make your expedition when the tide is ebbing and start the 3-mile return trip shortly after the tide begins to turn. The beach is narrow in places, and when the tide comes in, it can be challenging to make your way back to the parking area.

To get here, park at the North Beach County Park parking area and head west (left) for approximately forty-five minutes (depending on your pace) until you reach Glass Beach. You've arrived when you reach the area beneath a hundred-foot cliff with rusted-out car axles, which mark the spot like an X on a map.

Beach Glassing

Hunting for sea glass can be a surprising form of meditation. Walking slowly along a beach, scanning mounds of rocks for that little glint of aqua, that sanded piece of white camouflaged among the pebbles and sand, and that thrilling flash of rare cobalt blue that commands your attention—all of this can put you in a happy trance. It can also make you wonder what it was before the sea and surf transformed it—a mason jar, a beer bottle, a milk glass cold cream jar, a fancy china cup or saucer?

While removing rocks and shells from the beach is usually prohibited, glass is yours for the taking. It makes a lovely (and free) souvenir of your trip to the shore. It is a true hidden treasure, and it requires sharp eyes to spot the subtle colors peeking through the sand and seaweed. The best locations are near towns that may have been used as dumping spots at one point. Glass Beach near Port Townsend, the beach at Coupeville, Golden Gardens and Alki Beach in Seattle—don't be surprised if you find a rare piece of beach glass poking up through the sand.

The best times to look for beach glass are after intense storms and at low tide. Look higher up on the beach rather than the shoreline, among rocks and pebbles. White, clear, brown, and green shards are the most common, while blue, red, orange, and other vibrant colors are more prized by collectors. Make jewelry or a wind chime with your treasures, or simply put them in a glass hurricane vase or bowl.

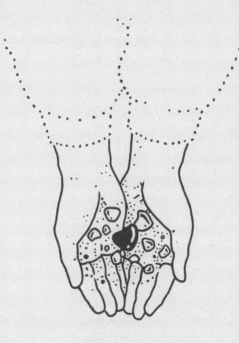

Fay Bainbridge Park

Building a fort of any kind is a childhood highlight. You can relive that glorious experience at this scenic beach by building a driftwood fort within view of Mount Rainier. The size of driftwood that washes up here is perfect for such an endeavor. Once you've built the beach house of your dreams, take a kayak out for a glide on the Salish Sea. Kayaks are free to borrow from a rack at the north entrance of the parking lot.

In addition to amusements for your inner child, this beach has amusements for *actual* children. Conditions are ideal for kite flying, and a playground in the shape of a pirate ship beckons the young and young at heart. But there's more, including picnic tables and volleyball courts, as well as opportunities for camping.

KNOW-HOW: If you decide to take out a loaner kayak, please be advised that these crafts are not inspected for seaworthiness and are to be used at your own risk.

Richmond
Beach

Carkeek
Park

Golden
Gardens

Myrtle
Edwards

Alki
Beach

~
Seattle
Beaches
~

SEATTLE BEACHES

50   Richmond Beach

53   Carkeek Park

56   Golden Gardens Park

59   Myrtle Edwards Park

60   Alki Beach

Seattle's beaches provide the city's inhabitants with a deeper connection to its greatest asset—an abundance of stunning scenery. In Seattle it seems that everywhere you look, there is a shimmer of water. It's easy to take such beauty for granted. A little bit of quality time at a beach can help you appreciate it with new eyes.

Richmond Beach

This beach lies at the foot of a steep cliffside that used to be a gravel mine. Before that endeavor reshaped this landscape, the beach was a Duwamish harvesting ground known as *q'q'e'waidet* (k-eh k-EH wai dut) for a tobacco-like plant that grew along the shoreline. A 10-foot-tall sculpture aptly titled *Welcoming Figure* greets you when you arrive at the beach. The piece is in the Coast Salish style and depicts a man and a woman with friendly faces, looking out over the Sound. The beach itself is a lovely combination of sand and driftwood. Pick a spot to cozy up with a book or simply take in the peaceful scenery. In late summer, bring a bucket and long-sleeved clothing to pick wild blackberries from the bushes lining the beach.

KNOW-HOW: There is ample signage indicating that pets must be leashed, but there is an area to the south of the beach entrance where locals bring their furry companions to enjoy each other's company untethered. This is unofficial, and circumstances are always a factor, so use your discernment.

Carkeek Park

If you visit on a clear day, you'll be treated to stunning views of the Olympic Mountains. You may also be entertained by the antics of the many crows who live in the trees just above the beach. It can be amusing just to sit and watch them act out their dramas.

In addition to these playful feathered residents, the park features picnic areas, public restrooms, a playground (with a salmon-shaped slide!), an educational center, and an extensive network of trails that span the 220 acres of green space maintained by Carkeek Park. This beach is a wonderful place to enjoy the sound of gentle waves and to skip a rock out into the glittering horizon.

KNOW-HOW: This beach is a favorite among locals who want to get out into the fresh air with their children and their fur babies, so be prepared to brave the crowds and search for parking. Also, be aware that this beach is only accessible via a railway overpass.

Flotsam and Jetsam

If something is jettisoned into the sea, it's called *jetsam*. Floating jetsam becomes *flotsam*, while jetsam that sinks is called *lagan*. Depending on the beachcomber and the object, jetsam that washes up on shore is either treasure or trash.

With so many human-made objects making their way into the sea, it is increasingly common to find artifacts of the Anthropocene along our beaches. Over the decades overturned ships have surrendered all kinds of strange goods to the waves, including rubber duckies, LEGOs, and telephones shaped like Garfield the cat. More commonly you'll find food wrappers and bottle caps.

While most beaches have a "leave-no-trace" guideline, feel free to take anything plastic, glass, or metal that doesn't belong to the earth. Removing trash is a simple act of stewardship that preserves the magnificent beauty of our shorelines and may even save a shorebird's life.

Golden Gardens Park

A few minutes northwest of Ballard lies a city park with something for every kind of beachgoer. Lush lawns provide a perfect place to enjoy a picnic or some quiet time with a favorite book. Benches offer a nice place to take in the scenic views and watch the sailboats on Shilshole Bay. At the north end of the beach you'll find designated firepits where you can cozy up to watch a fireside sunset.

There are swings and volleyball pits for playful beachgoers, though you'll need to bring your own ball and net. This beach also provides a perfect setting for kite flying, drone piloting, and metal detecting. If you dig, be sure to leave no trace. For pet lovers, the park boasts one of the best-loved off-leash areas in Seattle. There is ample space for your pooch to run and play, and there is a trail that connects the dog park with the beach.

KNOW-HOW: If you want to get out on the water, there are kayak and paddleboard rentals, as well as private boat charters and a boat ramp south of the park entrance. There are designated parking areas for boat trailers, as well as plenty of parking for regular vehicles.

Myrtle Edwards Park

This waterfront recreation area in the heart of downtown Seattle features Pocket Beach, a charming and aptly named little section of shoreline. At Pocket Beach you can enjoy the glitter of cityscapes and waves all at once. The space skillfully fuses the beauty of nature with the beauty of art, utility, and architecture.

From here you'll have views of the Space Needle and the P-I Globe, shining nostalgically behind paths dotted with trees and eye-catching public art. To the south you'll see industrial cranes looming like steel giraffes over West Seattle shipyards. Take a seat on one of the pieces of driftwood along the beach and search the horizon for the fins of orcas as the ferries make their slow glide across the bay. This beach is more of an immersion than a getaway. The paved paths are great for dog walkers, runners, and bicyclists.

KNOW-HOW: There are two ways to access this park. A pedestrian bridge on Third Street offers moderately easy access to parking—but be aware that there are stairs. The second option is to park somewhere near the intersection of Elliott and Broad and enter by way of the Elliott Bay Trail, which runs along the perimeter of Olympic Sculpture Park.

Alki Beach

This sandy destination is a lovely place to stroll with a sweetheart or take a break from the city routine. It's a short drive from downtown, but as you look across the bay at Seattle's iconic cityscape, you'll feel miles away from it all. The water is crystal clear, and the sand is soft. Fires are permitted, and you'll likely encounter the unexpected scent of smoke mingled in with the sound of waves and laughter. Several restaurants and bars line the beach, providing beachside refreshment, and there is a long, flat beach walk where you can enjoy jogging or walking your dog.

Due to its placement on Duwamish Peninsula, Alki Beach has a long history of welcoming visitors to its shores. As noted on the Seattle.gov website, on a stormy November day in 1851, Alki Beach became the historic landing site of the first whites to arrive in what is now Seattle. The Duwamish tribe, led by Chief Si'ahl, greeted the party and helped them build a cabin to survive the cold winter.

KNOW-HOW: There is a fine of up to $500 for pets on the beach. Volleyball courts are available but require reservations, which can be made by calling (206) 684-7204. The fee is $8 per hour, and players must bring their own net and ball. Schedule well in advance.

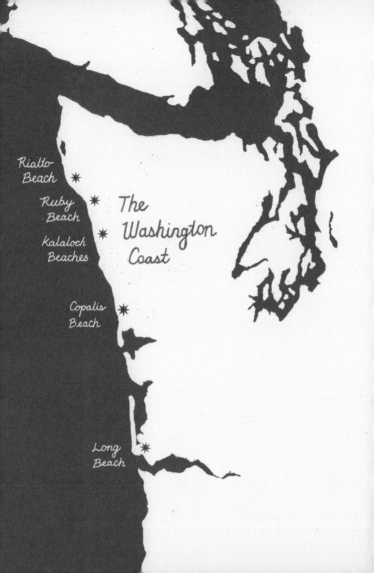

Rialto
Beach ✳

Ruby ✳
Beach

Kalaloch
Beaches

The
Washington
Coast

Copalis ✳
Beach

Long ✳
Beach

THE WASHINGTON COAST

64	Rialto Beach	73	Copalis Beach
67	Ruby Beach	74	Long Beach
70	Kalaloch Beaches		

The ocean beaches of Washington State are wild, moody, magnificent, and awe-inspiring. Depending on the weather, a beach visit can be a tumult of wind and waves or a sun-kissed bliss. At both extremes and every point in between, there is always plenty to do and see. From kite flying to beach driving, there are myriad ways to enjoy beach time.

Ocean Shores and Long Beach allow the operation of motor vehicles, but if you decide you'd like to drive on the beach, steer clear of soft "sugar" sand and be aware of streams and tides. The dynamic conditions of an oceanside can change rapidly, and you might find yourself stuck. If a tow truck reaches your vehicle before the tide, it's likely to cost upwards of $100. Always proceed with caution and be aware of pedestrians. The speed limit is 25 miles per hour.

Rialto Beach

When the road through the quiet stillness of the rain forest opens up to a shimmering vista, the first thing you might notice is that the ocean here is a roaring and unrelenting entity. The shoreline is a magical boundary between the world of people and the sea. While the tranquility of one beach may fill you with peace and the vastness of another may make you feel tiny, this beach inspires awe and gratitude for the beautiful living world.

Eagles chirp from treetops. A fallen forest of massive driftwood rests at the high tide line. Incoming waves spread a sizzling blanket of sea foam across the beach's black rocks. The sound dissipates and is replaced by the clatter of new waves. This beach is ideal for the nature hiker, the solitary adventurer, shutterbugs, and the quiet reflectors who like to loaf and enjoy the view.

KNOW-HOW: A 3-mile hike to the north will take you past colorful tide pools to a picturesque rock feature known simply as Hole-in-the-Wall, an opening in a wall of rock that you can walk through at low tide to the beach on the other side. If you plan on making this hike, be sure to check the tides before leaving to avoid being stranded at high tide. Looking south from the parking area's beach entrance, you'll see La Push, home to Quileute Nation. It's important to respect the boundary between the public beach and the section reserved by the Quileute in the Treaty of Olympia.

Ruby Beach

This beach is a dynamic and undulating landscape with a wide array of things to look at and interact with. Rugged sea stacks stand majestically, engulfed in ocean mist, sempiternal against the ever-frothing ocean. The beach underfoot changes every twenty paces. One minute you're navigating a tangle of driftwood, and the next, you're on fine pebbles that give way to soft sand, only to shift to cobblestones ten steps down the beach.

If you're lucky, you might come across a section of shore composed of the red, ruby-like granules from which the beach takes its name. This place feels radiant and alive with unnameable energy. It's one of the most photogenic beaches on the Washington coast. Be sure to bring your camera to capture the stunning scenery.

KNOW-HOW: A stream to the ocean cuts the beach in two. If you want to explore the driftwood trove on the northern section of Ruby Beach, you'll need to wade across the stream, so be sure to come prepared and dress appropriately. Wear shorts and bring along a pair of flip-flops or water shoes to protect your feet from the rocky streambed.

Beach Party

For untold ages these pebbles, here have danced
twirling in the clamor of waves, softening in the surf,
each turn and flourish, a patient, passionate churn
of advances and retreats, timed to the music of tides.

Twirling in the clamor of waves, softening in the surf,
each stone has a history—its own slow story of origin,
of advances and retreats, timed to the music of tides,
arisen from the molten earth, to break away anew.

Each stone has a history—its own slow story of origin,
millions of years to begin, millions more to end,
arisen from the molten earth, to break away anew,
free to tumble and roll, untethered, but never alone.

Millions of years to begin, millions more to end,
on the shore with millions of friends and time to spend,
free to tumble and roll, untethered, but never alone,
at this effervescent party where water touches land,

on the shore with millions of friends and time to spend,
each turn and flourish, a patient, passionate churn
at this effervescent party where water touches land—
for untold ages these pebbles, here have danced.

Kalaloch Beaches

The pull-off to Kalaloch Beach 1 provides access to parking and camping with proximity to the beach. You can park for an afternoon or take advantage of the excellent accommodations at South Beach Campground. If you're lucky, you can snag one of the few select sites that offer an ocean view from your tent.

From the shelter and privacy of your campsite, watch the sunset on the horizon and fall asleep to the soothing sound of waves. When you wake, take your travel mug for a stroll down a short trail and enjoy your morning coffee on a beautiful wave-swept beach.

Explore all the beaches along this 5-mile stretch of highway and see which is your favorite. If sandcastles and beach fires are your jam, you'll enjoy Beach 2, which features a wide sandy beach, while Beaches 3 and 4 offer unique rock formations and tide pools rich with life and color.

KNOW-HOW: While you're here, be sure to visit the Tree of Life. This tree is an impressive anomaly of nature. Suspended in the cliffside above nothing but empty space, the exposed roots form a shallow cave. You can walk under the tangled root system and observe nature's intricate handiwork. Don't skip this one-of-a-kind sight. Find it by following the trail down from the Kalaloch Campground parking lot and turning right when you get to the beach. The tree is a short distance from the foot of the trail.

Copalis Beach

This beach is massive, lovely, wide, and long. The sand here is (mostly) firm enough to drive on, and with the exception of a pedestrian-friendly area, driving is allowed year-round. In fact, one section of the beach functions as Washington State Route 109. If you don't want to brave the beach in your car, you can always race remote control vehicles down the long straightaways.

Another fun fact about this slice of oceanside is that it hosts the only beach airstrip in the Lower 48. Of course, a beach large enough to land a plane gives visitors a true sense of Earth's vastness and grandeur. Experiencing this landscape for the first time can reveal a surprising sense of scale. You might feel tiny. You might find yourself walking for a long time toward a landmark or another person without gaining much ground.

KNOW-HOW: Try visiting during the Festival of Colors to see a flock of kites shining their bright hues against the sky. Razor clam digging is permitted when conditions are safe and clams are in season. Beach fires are also allowed as long as it isn't excessively windy and the fire is less than 3 feet in diameter and under 3 feet tall, and not built on shellfish beds. Swimming is not recommended.

Long Beach

An arch over Bolstad Avenue's entrance proudly proclaims "World's Longest Beach." Approximately 20 miles of the 28-mile beach make up the longest stretch of drivable beach in the world. You can ride your bike along the paved 8-mile scenic route that Lewis and Clark traversed more than two hundred years ago.

Long Beach is also home to the World Kite Museum and Hall of Fame. There is something whimsical and uplifting about the sight of hundreds of kites sailing their colors against the backdrop of a blue sky. In addition to kites, you might see how many kinds of shorebirds you can spot. Buffleheads, whimbrels, pintails, and snowy plovers are only a few among the more than 150 types of birds found here. Due to dangerous conditions, swimming is prohibited, and maintaining a close watch over children and pets is advised.

KNOW-HOW: Long Beach is home to the Razor Clam Festival, which kicked off in 1940 with thousands of visitors showing up to dig clams. Some of that clam harvest would become "the world's largest clam fritter," which was cooked up in "the world's largest frying pan." It's said that girls skated on large slabs of butter to grease the pan, and cooks used hoes and square shovels to maneuver the fritter.

The Changer and the Gossips

A long, *long* time ago, before the world became what it is today, the Changer was traveling around seeing what needed to be changed. One of his favorite places was the ocean shore. He loved to relax at the seaside, but he soon noticed that whenever he was enjoying the glitter of the waves at the turn of the tide, there would always appear groups of little people, gossiping, just gossiping about each other and every little thing. They would grin from ear to ear after repeating their juicy scuttlebutt.

The Changer was annoyed and tried to move along to a new stretch of sandy shore, but every beach he went to was filled with these gossiping beings. He warned them to quit their chatter, but instead of stopping, they whispered under their breath. "Psst," they would say. "Psst, did you hear?" "Psst. Psst. Psst. Did you hear?" Their whispering and gossip were everywhere.

"This whispering is even worse than all that gossip said out loud!" said the Changer. "You have one last chance to stop it now." And so, the little gossiping people stopped . . . but only for a little while.

Before long, they were back at it again. "Psst, did you hear? Psst. Guess what I heard."

Finally, the Changer had had enough. With a sweep of his arms, he gathered up all the little gossips and changed them into clams, with their big mouths smiling from ear to ear. He cast them out into the waves and covered them with the tide so he wouldn't have to hear their clamor anymore.

You can still sometimes see them today at the turn of the tide, spouting water, still sharing their juicy gossip. "Psst. Psst. Did you hear?" They're still there, grinning from ear to ear, deep beneath the sand. And that's the story of the Changer and the gossips.

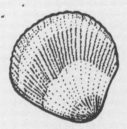

Wreck of the
Peter Iridale ✳

Seaside ✳

Cannon Beach ✳

Manzanita ✳

Depoe Bay ✳

The
Oregon
Coast

Cobble Beach ✳

Agate Beach ✳

Hobbit Beach ✳

Heceta Head
Lighthouse ✳

Sunset Bay
State Park ✳

THE OREGON COAST

80	Wreck of the *Peter Iredale*
85	Seaside Beach
86	Cannon Beach
91	Manzanita
94	Depoe Bay
97	Cobble Beach
98	Agate Beach
103	Hobbit Beach
104	Heceta Head Lighthouse
109	Sunset Bay State Park

Highlights of the Oregon coast include the Wreck of the *Peter Iredale* at Fort Stevens State Park, Yaquina Head Lighthouse at Cobble Beach in Newport, and Haystack Rock at Cannon Beach. Cannon Beach is also home to the annual Cannon Beach Sandcastle Contest.

While Oregon's top-notch beaches are the highlight of the coast, there are also various roadside attractions. If you're making a road trip, be sure to stop in at Cape Perpetua Scenic Area and check out Thor's Well and the Spouting Horn. There are also many sporadic parking areas with trails leading to smaller beaches that are perfect for a quick stretch and picnic.

Wreck of the *Peter Iredale*

Twenty minutes west of Astoria, you'll find big waves and all the expected scenery of an ocean beach. You'll also find an extra feature that you won't find anywhere else: the *Peter Iredale* shipwreck. In October of 1906, a storm tossed the ship and her crew onto the shore where the hull now rests. Fortunately, none of the crew were lost and the cargo hold was empty, but the ship itself was stranded and is slowly being reclaimed by the ocean.

From the tall banks above the sandy shoreline, the wreck doesn't look like much, but at low tide you can walk right up to the bones of the hull and see what an impressive structure it must have been to endure more than a hundred years in the ocean waves.

KNOW-HOW: Fort Stevens State Park features well-maintained public restrooms, picnic areas, campsites, and parking lots near the beach for easy access. Enjoy this park as a day trip or a weekend getaway. The campgrounds are clean and generously spaced out. Yurts are available, and there is a section of the park for RVs. There is even a first-come-first-serve loop in the campground.

Shipwrecks

On the Oregon and Washington coasts, sailing can be anything but smooth. Powerful currents, strong winds, thick fog, and a massive underwater sandbar make for a treacherous patch of ocean known as the Graveyard of the Pacific. The Columbia Bar is an underwater sandbar at the mouth of the Columbia River. It spans 3 miles wide and stretches 6 miles out to sea. Since documentation began in 1792, it has claimed more than two thousand vessels and over seven hundred lives.

The Beeswax Shipwreck is one of the oldest known shipwrecks in the region. Researchers believe it to be the Spanish ship *Santo Cristo de Burgos*, which went missing in 1693. They theorize that the shipwreck washed ashore after a tsunami sometime around 1700. Though the wreck itself has still not been located, beeswax and shards of Chinese porcelain have been washing up on the shores near Manzanita for centuries. Some of the nearly fifteen thousand shards were used to make arrowheads, and a fur trader's journals from 1813 note that members of the Clatsop tribe were trading immense quantities of beeswax in Astoria. When asked where it came from, they said that it was from the shipwreck near Nehalem Bay.

Seaside Beach

People flock to this beach for the gorgeous, expansive shoreline, which offers fluffy golden sand and quintessential beach experiences such as sunbathing, kite flying, and sandcastle building. Don't worry, though. While you'll certainly never have the place to yourself, there's plenty of beach to go around. The beach is wide enough to accommodate crowds without feeling crowded.

Fun fact: People gather here annually to welcome runners on the last leg of the Hood to Coast Relay. Also known as the Mother of All Relays, the race has sold out for thirty years straight and draws participants from over forty countries worldwide. Teams of twelve pass the baton along a 199-mile route starting on Mount Hood and concluding with fanfare on Seaside's beach.

KNOW-HOW: In Seaside the streets are lined with a surprising array of hotels, restaurants, and attractions to accommodate the many guests who visit the beach and the Seaside Civic and Convention Center throughout the year.

Cannon Beach

The exciting feature of this beach is Haystack Rock. This impressive geological anomaly was formed by lava flows over fifteen million years ago. It stands 235 feet tall (approximately 17 stories) and can be seen from Highway 101. Because of its height, it's the perfect place for tufted puffins and other seabirds to build their nests out of reach of land-based predators. Climbing is prohibited to protect visitors from being stranded as well as to protect seabirds from feeling threatened.

Another exciting feature of Haystack Rock emerges at low tide: a tide pool and its fragile panoply of life. Tide pool creatures are easily injured, so walking on sand and bare rocks is the best way to avoid squishing any living creatures. (See the Tide Pools section to learn more about how to enjoy these delicate ecosystems, page 114.)

KNOW-HOW: Cannon Beach offers lodging, charming restaurants, breweries, boutiques, gift shops, public restrooms, and even public transportation. The northern beaches feature a bird estuary and quiet rental cottages, while everything from Haystack Rock south is bustling and touristy. If you're staying the night, be sure to check websites like Vrbo.com and Airbnb.com. Many ocean-view vacation homes are available through the web.

Dramatic Geology of the Oregon Coast

Tall as a seventeen-story building and towering over the town of Cannon Beach, Haystack Rock is one of the most famous geological features of the Oregon coast—but where did it come from? This monolith, along with other unique coastal rock formations, came into being more than fifteen million years ago.

At that time lava flows from the Yellowstone hotspot spread fiery fingers across the region. Geologists believe that it took less than a week for lava flows to travel 300 miles to the coast, where they tunneled through softer sediments and re-erupted on the sea floor as "submarine" (or secondary) volcanoes. The throats of these volcanoes cooled, hardened, and spent millions of years submerged in the ocean.

It has only been a few million years, give or take, since they were pushed up toward the surface by a process called tectonic uplift, which occurs when one plate sub-ducts under another, causing the latter to rise and reveal the secrets of Earth's volatile past.

Manzanita

There is something about seeing ocean waves roll in that is like watching a magic trick. It feels carefully orchestrated for your enjoyment. One of the most spectacular places to glimpse this magic is at Neahkahnie Viewpoint, a few miles north of Manzanita. This mountainside lookout offers breathtaking views of the ocean and beaches below.

As you make your way toward town, you'll be delighted to discover that Neahkahnie Beach is just as beautiful at sea level. If you go while the tide is ebbing, you'll see a luminous sheen of seawater atop the perfectly flat, dense sand, creating a vast mirror serenely reflecting the sky.

An enjoyable way to interact with this landscape is to take off your shoes and wade. It's a lovely feeling to stand still as a wave engulfs your ankles and retreats, pulling the sand in swirls from beneath your feet. Neahkahnie Beach is only a mile north of Manzanita but feels quieter and more isolated than the beach at the western edge of town.

KNOW-HOW: The town of Manzanita is a charming hippie haven. If you decide you'd like to stay awhile, there are hotels, but camping is your better bet. Nehalem Bay State Park is a five-minute drive from town and offers a campground, amphi-theater, meeting hall, boat ramp, picnic areas, beach access, and trails for horseback riding.

Beach Glass

Here, in this luminous landscape, vivid as we go,
each gleaming shard is softened, gently as it rolls
along a silky stretch of sand, soft between our toes.
Our footsteps break a silver surface, a foggy bit of glass,

each gleaming shard is softened, gently as it rolls.
Bottle green seaweed twirls around our ankles.
Our footsteps break a silver surface, a foggy bit of glass
softened like me, by its time in the sea,

bottle-green seaweed twirls around our ankles.
This soft-edged relic begun as sand, returning to sand,
softened like me, by its time in the sea,
no longer meant to carry or enclose, but simply to be.

This soft-edged relic, begun as sand, returning to sand,
the secret of its journey, now the only thing it holds;
no longer meant to carry or enclose, but simply to be.
A fiery forge, a given shape, things cut, things contained,

the secret of its journey, now the only thing it holds,
along a silky stretch of sand, soft between our toes.
A fiery forge, a given shape, things cut, things contained,
here, in this luminous landscape, vivid as we go.

Depoe Bay

If you pause here along your way, you may be joining dozens of other visitors who've come to catch a glimpse of migrating whales. You'll also enjoy nature's ostentatious display of gigantic waves crashing against the cliffside. The waves during a king tide create an awe-inspiring sight, and the boom of the surf is thrilling. At the golden hour, when the sun has begun its descent toward the horizon, the whole place is sometimes bathed in a glowing haze created by light caught in mist made of shattered waves.

At the head of the bridge, you'll find the Depoe Bay Whale Watching Center, where you can get in out of the weather and try to spot the heart-shaped spouts of gray whales. The center will even lend you a pair of binoculars.

KNOW-HOW: This little town is situated atop an oceanside cliff with pull-in parking directly off the highway. You can schedule whale-watching tours with one of the companies along this main street.

Cobble Beach

Picturesque is the first word that comes to mind when describing the Yaquina Head Lighthouse at Cobble Beach. As beautiful as the lighthouse is, it's merely a backdrop to the magnificent and fascinating sights at Cobble Beach. The beach itself is composed of smooth black cobblestones that make a pleasing clacking, cascading sound at the tide's turn.

At low tide you can visit tide pools that glitter with color and life. (See the Tide Pools section for guidelines on how to safely enjoy these fragile marine gardens, page 114.) Seals sun themselves on nearby rocks, and if you stay until sunset, Mother Nature will treat you to a world-class light show.

KNOW-HOW: The cost to enter the park in a personal passenger vehicle is $7 for a three-day pass. Entry allows access to Cobble Beach, and during regular operating hours, it includes ranger-led lighthouse tours and entrance into the interpretive center. The Bureau of Land Management recommends that you stop in at the visitor's center to learn how to fully and safely enjoy the park.

Agate Beach

At Agate Beach you'll find soft sand, and plenty of it. This is an expansive and easily accessible beach, excellent for dog walking, kite flying, drone piloting, picnicking, surfing, metal detecting, and razor clam digging. Beach fires are allowed for most of the year, so cozying up to watch a sunset here is an excellent option. There are plenty of nearby restaurants, hotels, and shops to visit, and if you're a seafood lover, you'll want to enjoy the catch of the day at one of the many restaurants along Newport's Historic Bayfront.

KNOW-HOW: The beach is situated just off Highway 101 and accessible via a short pedestrian path through a tunnel underneath the old highway. The large parking area includes access to public restrooms and spaces for trailers.

Beach Fire

Measure wealth by how well you enjoy the hours
fluttering by in praise of sunshine and the ocean breeze,
whispering love songs across waves that kiss the beach.
This wealth takes work, and absolutely no work at all.

Fluttering by in praise of sunshine and the ocean breeze,
don't mistake leisure for laziness. This gratitude is rigorous.
This wealth takes work, and absolutely no work at all.
This gift of a moment, to be alive, to feel at peace . . .

don't mistake leisure for laziness. This gratitude is rigorous.
To be filled up and satisfied by a day at the beach,
this gift of a moment, to be alive, to feel at peace,
it means your heart-fire flames a lovely heat,

to be filled up and satisfied by a day at the beach.
You could toast marshmallows by that warmth,
it means your heart-fire flames a lovely heat,
the glowing embers, a boundless source of power,

you could toast marshmallows by that warmth,
whispering love songs across waves that kiss the beach,
the glowing embers, a boundless source of power.
Measure wealth by how well you enjoy the hours.

Hobbit Beach

This beach is a stunner. Arguably one of the most beautiful places on Earth. When you emerge onto the glistening shore, you'll feel like you've stepped back in time or into another universe, and a better one at that. The pristine sand stretches along the edge of a cliff face engulfed in trees. You'd never know that traffic raced along a highway a half-mile away. If it weren't for a reflective sign marking the trailhead, you might have a hard time finding your way back.

If you bring snacks and a blanket, you can enjoy the serenity of this oceanside treasure with a day of picnics and naps. Let the roar of the ocean clear your mind while you soak up some vitamin D from the delicious rays of the sun.

KNOW-HOW: To get here you'll need to park at the Hobbit Beach trailhead and make a little half-mile hike down the aptly named trail through a lush tunnel of twisting foliage that glows every shade of green under the sun. You'll need to be surefooted and keep your eye on the terrain, as there are a lot of exposed tree roots to catch your foot. Wear good shoes.

Heceta Head Lighthouse

The Heceta Head Lighthouse is the brightest light on the Oregon coast. It shines a beam observable from 21 nautical miles away (24 miles). The land where the lighthouse stands is part of the Siuslaw people's traditional homelands, who enjoyed the abundant fishing and hunting available in this area. There is a beach at the edge of the parking lot, where you can enjoy a quiet moment watching for whales or the many sea lions that frequent this area.

Fun fact: A little over a mile south of the lighthouse, along Highway 101, is the entrance to Sea Lion Caves, a system of caves that are the longest in the United States.

KNOW-HOW: Heceta Head is a popular stop along the Oregon coast, so be prepared to brave the crowds. To get to the lighthouse, you'll need to purchase a daily parking pass and make the short half-mile hike up a gravel pathway to the scenic seascapes at the top of the trail. The path is well maintained and smooth enough to accommodate strollers and wheelchairs. Partway up you'll find the lighthouse keeper's quarters, now used as a bed-and-breakfast. There is also a gift shop near the top.

Lighthouse Lodging

What do you love most about a lighthouse? Is it the jeweled Fresnel lens, the spiral staircase, the view of a sparkling seascape? Whatever your favorite lighthouse feature, you can enjoy its special magic during an overnight stay. In recent years many lighthouses throughout Washington and Oregon have been outfitted to accommodate overnight guests. Here is a list of some fine offerings available to rent overnight.

POINT NO POINT LIGHTHOUSE is a spectacular scenic destination located at the tip of the Kitsap Peninsula. It offers beautiful views of Mount Baker, Mount Rainier, and the Seattle skyline.

POINT ROBINSON LIGHTHOUSE on Vashon Island has two Keepers' Quarters available for overnight use. Both cottages feature views of the water and all the amenities of home.

NORTH HEAD LIGHTHOUSE in Cape Disappointment State Park has three houses available for overnight rental. Each house can accommodate up to six guests.

POINT WILSON LIGHTHOUSE at picturesque Fort Worden State Park has lodging for eight and is located only minutes from the charming seaside town of Port Townsend.

HECETA HEAD LIGHTHOUSE near Yachats, Oregon, is open year-round as a bed-and-breakfast offering a seven-course breakfast and a wine and cheese social.

You can reserve each of these lighthouse getaways and many others by visiting the United States Lighthouse Society and searching accommodations by states and provinces at this link: www.uslhs.org/fun/lighthouse -accommodations.

Sunset Bay State Park

As the name suggests, the beach at Sunset Bay State Park is a beautiful place to watch the sun make its dunk into the horizon. But that's not all this location has to offer. The sandy beach is a perfect crescent, protected by cliffs on both sides and a natural breakwater of picturesque rocks. The tall cliffs and the breakwater make the bay swimmer friendly and good for stand-up paddleboarding or kayaking. Another interesting effect of the natural breakwater is that you can hear the waves breaking twice: once when they roar in from the ocean to crash against the rocks, and again as they tumble up onto the sandy shore.

KNOW-HOW: If you visit at low tide, you'll be able to see the intricate root systems of trees that were covered with water more than fifteen hundred years ago. Geologists initially believed that the submerged trees were the result of an earthquake, but recent studies show that they gradually inched their way into the sea. The beach is accessible by a day-use parking area, or via a well-maintained trail leading from an equally well-maintained campground.

SAFETY AND GUIDELINES

Unfamiliar marine environments present hazards that may be beyond your control or awareness. For optimal enjoyment, always observe beach signage and follow safety guidelines. Observe posted restrictions on shellfish harvesting, metal detecting, pets, drones, fires, and other activities that may negatively impact the environment, as well as others.

To avoid unanticipated hazards, never access areas reserved for restricted use or beaches marked as private property unless you have attained the required permissions.

Camping

One of the finest ways to enjoy a beach getaway is to unplug at a nearby campsite. Plan your trip at the following websites for Oregon and Washington State Parks.

- Washington State Parks: Washington.GoingtoCamp .com
- Oregon State Parks: StateParks.Oregon.gov

Ferries

Washington State Ferries provide easy access to some of the most beautiful destinations on the planet. The ferry ride itself can be a nice little transition from regular life to beach life. During peak season it can be challenging to board a ferry without a reservation. Don't let long lines spoil your trip. Visit their website for more information and to purchase tickets: WSDOT.wa.gov/Ferries.

Nature and Wildlife

The beaches of the Pacific Northwest are host to an array of life forms. Many of the most visited beaches are also designated as protected habitats and marine gardens, so follow posted protocols for interactions with tide pools and landscapes. Collection of any plants, animals, or shells is prohibited, but you can take as many pictures as you like.

Parking

Automobile access to many of the finest beaches in Washington requires the purchase and display of a Discover Pass. Day passes are available for $10 per day, or you can purchase an annual pass for $30. Visit this website for details: DiscoverPass.wa.gov.

Pets

Most beaches described in this book allow pets, but it's crucial to observe leash laws, primarily to protect wildlife. There are many places where seabirds make their nests, and disturbing them could mean life or death for their chicks.

Shellfish

Harvesting shellfish can be a wonderful way to spend a day at the beach. Always observe harvesting seasons, as well as harvest sizes and limits. To learn more about how to attain a license and harvest safely, visit the website for the Department of Fish and Wildlife in the appropriate state.

Streams

In their long journey from the mountains, small creeks travel across many different landscapes before cutting their paths across beaches to reach the sea. Because toxins may have been picked up along the way, do not interact with these seemingly harmless waterways.

Swimming

Swimming is one of the best ways to enjoy a beach. Please note, none of the beaches in this book employ a lifeguard, so safety is 100 percent the responsibility of beachgoers. Always observe safety above all things. If you plan on swimming, research posted guidelines of the beach you're going to visit.

Whether or not you plan to swim, it's important to understand that the ocean is temperamental. Many beaches post warnings about "sneaker waves," which can swell higher up along the shore than anticipated and sweep people or pets out to sea. Swimmers should maintain a safe distance from logs and other floating debris.

Long Beach prohibits swimming, while several other ocean beaches strongly advise against it. The calmer waters of the Olympic Peninsula and the San Juan Islands are much more hospitable to swimming. However, cold temperatures in this region make hypothermia a risk, and wearing a life jacket is recommended during colder weather.

Tide Pools

These colorful marine gardens display a swaying plenitude of fragile intertidal life. The best guidance here is to explore gently. While many tide pool creatures will survive if you touch them lightly, others should only be observed with your eyes. Mind restricted areas and don't remove any rocks. If you move seaweed to view creatures, please replace it after you've had a peek, so that anything living underneath will remain protected. Many areas that feature tide pools offer interpretive exhibits that provide a wealth of information on how to enjoy a tide pool and minimize your impact while visiting.

Tides

Maintain an awareness of tides. In other words, stay alert! There are areas such as Glass Beach (North Beach County Park) and Hole-in-the-Wall (Rialto Beach) where you can become stranded due to a high tide obstructing access to your return path. Also, be aware that if you venture out onto tide flats, the tide can come in faster than anticipated, and you may end up racing against it.

In areas where you can drive on the beach, such as Copalis Beach (Ocean Shores) and Long Beach, it's imperative to stay aware of the tide to avoid accidentally stranding your vehicle. It's a good idea to check tide charts before hitting any beach.

ACTIVITIES BY AREA

Best Beach Glassing
- Glass Beach

Best Camping
- Deception Pass Campgrounds
- Kaloloch Beach/South Beach
- Dungeness Recreation Area

Best Driftwood Fort Building
- Ebey's Landing
- Fay Bainbridge Park

Best Geological Anomalies
- Sunset Bay State Park
- Cannon Beach
- Cobble Beach

Best Kite Flying
- Copalis Beach
- Long Beach

Best Lighthouses
- Lime Kiln
- Yaquina Point
- Heceta Head

Best Paddling
- Doe Bay
- Golden Gardens Park

Best Polar Bear Plunge
- Golden Gardens Park

Best Sandcastle Beaches
- Seaside Beach
- Cannon Beach

Best Tide Pooling
- Cannon Beach
- Cobble Beach
- Rialto Beach

Best Whale Watching
- Depoe Bay
- Lime Kiln Lighthouse
- Kalaloch Beach 2

RESOURCES

Books

- *By the Shore* by Nancy Blakey
- *Fylling's Illustrated Guide to Pacific Coast Tide Pools* by Marni Fylling
- *Moon Coastal Oregon* by Judy Jewell and W. C. McRae
- *The New Beachcomber's Guide to the Pacific Northwest* by J. Duane Sept

Organizations

- **Ocean Blue Project:** An Oregon-based nonprofit focused on ocean conservation
  OceanBlueProject.org

- **Surfrider Foundation Seattle Chapter:** A grassroots network protecting Washington beaches through letter-writing campaigns, water-quality improvement projects, and attendance at public hearings
  Seattle.Surfrider.org

- **Washington CoastSavers:** A volunteer group dedicated to keeping Washington beaches clean through beach cleanups and educational offerings
  CoastSavers.org

- **Washington Water Trails Association:** An organization protecting public access to Washington's shorelines, beaches, marine trails, parks, and campsites
  WWTA.org

ACKNOWLEDGMENTS

I owe immense gratitude to Jennifer Worick, Nicole Hardy, and Jane Hodges for my involvement in creating this book. I have loved answering the call to celebrate the splendor of my homelands through writing. I would also like to acknowledge the steadfast support I've received from my husband, Darryl Brubacher. He has accompanied me on much of this journey and contributed many hours as my driver, chef, and campsite coordinator.

Thank you to Lela Childs for accompanying me to the San Juan Islands, and to Jill McCabe Johnson and the Kangaroo House for their excellent hospitality. Finally, a huge *hy'sxw'qe* to Topsy Kinley, Renee Swan-Waite, Candice Wilson, and Jackie Ballew. Your encouragement is priceless.

The story "The Changer and the Gossips" was originally told to me by Smak i'ya' (Matt Warbus), who said it came down to him from Tsilixw, the late hereditary chief of the Lummi Nation.

All of the poems in this book are written in the pantoum format, with lines that repeat and roll through the poem like waves along a shoreline.

INDEX

A

Agate Beach, 98
Alki Beach, 44, 60

C

Cama Beach, 36
Cannon Beach, 79, 86, 88,
    116–117
Carkeek Park, 53
Cobble Beach, 79, 97,
    116–117
Copalis Beach, 73, 115–116
Coupeville, 29, 39, 44
Crescent Beach Preserve, 19

D

Deception Pass State Park,
    24
Depoe Bay, 94, 117
Doe Bay, 20, 117
Dungeness Spit, 39–40

E

Eagle Cove Beach, 9
Ebey's Landing, 30, 116
English Camp, 13

F

Fay Bainbridge Park, 39, 46,
    116
Fourth of July Beach, 10

G

Glass Beach, 39, 43–44,
    114, 116
Golden Gardens Park, 56,
    117

H

Heceta Head Lighthouse,
    104, 107
Hobbit Beach, 103

K

Kalaloch Beaches, 70,
116–117

L

Lime Kiln Lighthouse, 14,
117
Long Beach, 63, 74,
114–116

M

Manzanita, 82, 91
Myrtle Edwards Park, 59

R

Rialto Beach, 64, 114, 117
Richmond Beach, 50
Ruby Beach, 67

S

Seaside Beach, 85, 117
Semiahmoo Spit, 1–2
Sunset Bay State Park, 109,
116

W

Wreck of the *Peter Iredale*,
79–80

ABOUT THE AUTHOR

RENA PRIEST is a poet and an enrolled member of the Lhaq'temish (Lummi) Nation. She is the recipient of the 2020 Vadon Foundation Fellowship, an Allied Arts Foundation Professional Poets Award, and an American Book Award (2018). She is a National Geographic Explorer (2018–2020) and has been awarded residency fellowships from Hedgebrook, Hawthornden Castle, and Mineral School. Priest has published two poetry collections, with individual poems featured at Poets.org, *Poetry Northwest*, *A Dozen Nothing*, and elsewhere. Priest has also published nonfiction pieces in *High Country News*, *YES!* magazine, *Seattle Met*, *Adventures Northwest*, and *Nautilus*. Learn more at RenaPriest.com.

ABOUT THE ILLUSTRATOR

JAKE STOUMBOS is an illustrator and graphic designer based out of Seattle, Washington. His work is inspired by nature, skateboarding, and conversations with friends. To see more of Jake's work, visit his Instagram @curb.fruit, or find him online at JakeStoumbos.com.